by Ellen Lawrence

Consultants:

Suzy Gazlay, MA
Recipient, Presidential Award for Excellence in Science Teaching

Kimberly Brenneman, PhD
National Institute for Early Education Research, Rutgers University, New Brunswick, New Jersey

New York, New York

Credits

Cover © Robert Neumann/Shutterstock; 3, © Coramax/Shutterstock, © Lyudmyla Kharlamova/Shutterstock, and Markus Gann/Shutterstock; 4–5, © Marmi/Shutterstock, © Anatoliy Samara/Shutterstock, © KKulikov/Shutterstock, © Nikolajs Lunskijs/Shutterstock, © Yulia Glam/Shutterstock, and © Coramax/Shutterstock; 6–7, © Coramax/Shutterstock, © Blacknote/Shutterstock, © Palo_ok/Shutterstock, © ancroft/Shutterstock, and © Matthew Cole/Shutterstock; 8–9, © Coramax/Shutterstock, © urfin/Shutterstock, © Wolna/Shutterstock, © Ilona Baha/Shutterstock, and © Danny Smythe/Shutterstock; 10–11, © Coramax/Shutterstock, © Planner/Shutterstock, © jcjgphotography/Shutterstock, and © Ruby Tuesday Books; 12–13, © Coramax/Shutterstock, © Brittny/Shutterstock, © Sylverarts/Shutterstock, © Ingvar Bjork/Shutterstock, and © photosync/Shutterstock; 14–15, © Coramax/Shutterstock, © aopsan/Shutterstock, © Ensuper/Shutterstock, © bonchan/Shutterstock, © filmfoto/Shutterstock, © graja/Shutterstock, and © Markus Gann/Shutterstock; 16–17, © Coramax/Shutterstock, and © Igor Kovalchuk/Shutterstock; 18–19, Coramax/Shutterstock, © Dave Pressland/FLPA, and © Jurgen & Christine Sohns/FLPA; 20–21, © Coramax/Shutterstock, © Yulia Glam/Shutterstock, © esbobeldijk/Shutterstock, © Planner/Shutterstock, © Ruby Tuesday Books, © Shelby Allison/Shutterstock, and © Wild Arctic Pictures/Shutterstock; 22, © Ramona Heim/Shutterstock, © AlesHostnik/Shutterstock, © Svhl/Shutterstock, © Lars Granström/Shutterstock, © Denphumi/Shutterstock, and © Sergii Figurnyi/Shutterstock; 23, © Pichugin Dmitry/Shutterstock, © Coramax/Shutterstock, © Prezoom.nl/Shutterstock, © jcjgphotography/Shutterstock, © Margarita Borodina/Shutterstock, and © OlegDoroshin/Shutterstock; 24, Comramax/Shutterstock.

Publisher: Kenn Goin
Creative Director: Spencer Brinker
Design: Emma Randall
Photo Researcher: Ruby Tuesday Books Ltd.

Library of Congress Cataloging-in-Publication Data in process at time of publication (2013)
Library of Congress Control Number: 2012050812
ISBN-13: 978-1-61772-738-2 (library binding)

For more information, write to Bearport Publishing Company, Inc., 45 West 21st Street, Suite 3B, New York, New York 10010. Printed in the United States of America.

10 9 8 7 6 5 4 3 2 1

Contents

Let's Investigate Color. 4

What makes a rainbow? 6

Can different colors make things warmer? 8

How can we make new colors? 10

What makes up different colors? 12

How can we make colors lighter or darker? 14

How can we invent new colors? 16

How do animals use color to stay safe? 18

Discovery Time 20

Color in Your World. 22

Science Words. 23

Index. 24

Read More. 24

Learn More Online 24

About the Author 24

Let's Investigate Color

Look around your room. What colors do you see? You probably see so many different colors that it's difficult to list them all. That's because our world is filled with color. Now it's time to investigate color like a scientist. Inside this book are lots of fun experiments and cool facts about color. So grab a notebook, and let's start exploring!

Check It Out!

Most people stop and stare when they see the beautiful colors of a **rainbow** in the sky. Let's investigate the colors that make up a rainbow.

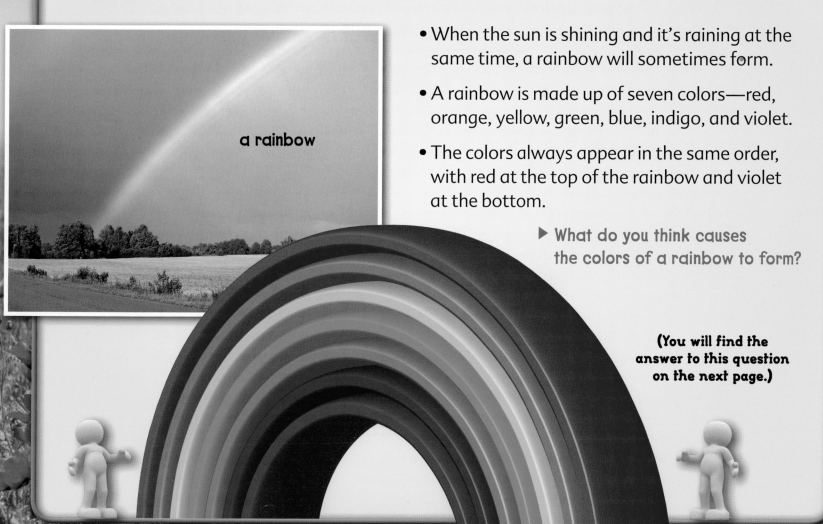

a rainbow

- When the sun is shining and it's raining at the same time, a rainbow will sometimes form.

- A rainbow is made up of seven colors—red, orange, yellow, green, blue, indigo, and violet.

- The colors always appear in the same order, with red at the top of the rainbow and violet at the bottom.

▶ What do you think causes the colors of a rainbow to form?

(You will find the answer to this question on the next page.)

5

What makes a rainbow?

Colorful rainbows form when sunlight shines through raindrops. Sunlight may not look colorful, but it's actually made up of seven colors. When sunlight passes through raindrops, the water bends the light. As the light bends, it splits into its different colors, which we see as a beautiful rainbow. Let's investigate to see how this happens.

You will need:

- A large piece of white paper
- A flashlight
- A box about ten inches (25 cm) high
- A glass of water (a plain glass with no pattern is best)
- A notebook and pencil
- Colored pencils

1 Lay a large piece of paper on the floor and shine a flashlight on it.

▶ What color is the light?

2 Now place a box at the edge of the paper, and stand a glass of water on top of it. The glass should be close to the edge of the box and above the end of the paper.

▶ What do you think will happen to the light if you shine it through the water?

▶ What might you see on the paper?

Write your **predictions** in your notebook.

6

3 Stand behind the box, and shine the flashlight through the water onto the paper.

▶ What color is the light on the paper?

In your notebook, write down what happened.

▶ What effect did the water have on the beam of light?

▶ Did you see any colors on the paper?

Draw a picture of what you saw using colored pencils.

▶ Do your predictions match what happened?

(To learn more about this investigation and find the answers to the questions, see pages 20–21.)

Can different colors make things warmer?

On a hot, sunny day, the color of your T-shirt can help you stay cool or make you hot. Why? Dark and light colors **absorb** different amounts of heat. If your T-shirt is a color that absorbs lots of heat, you will feel warm. If it's a color that does not absorb heat, it will help you stay cool. So which colors absorb the most heat—dark or light colors? Let's investigate!

You will need:

- Two sheets of construction paper— one white and one black
- Two glasses
- Two rubber bands
- A pitcher of water
- Two thermometers
- A notebook and pencil

 Roll a sheet of white paper and a sheet of black paper into tubes.

 Place each tube over a glass, and then hold the paper tube in place with a rubber band.

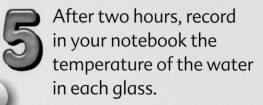

3 Fill each glass halfway with water. Put a **thermometer** into each glass of water. After a few minutes, check the thermometers and record in your notebook the **temperature** of the water in each glass.

5 After two hours, record in your notebook the temperature of the water in each glass.

4 Stand the glasses outside in a place where the sun will shine on them for two hours.

▶ Do you think the black or white paper will absorb the most heat from the sun? Why?

▶ What will happen to the water in that glass?

Write your predictions in your notebook.

▶ Which glass had the warmest water?

▶ Did the black or white paper absorb the most heat?

▶ Do your predictions match what happened?

▶ To stay cool, is it best to wear a light- or dark-colored T-shirt?

(To learn more about this investigation and find the answers to the questions, see pages 20–21.)

How can we make new colors?

When we paint pictures, we use different colored paints. We can even mix colors together to make brand new colors. For example, if you mix red and yellow paint, you get orange paint. Let's investigate how to mix two different colors together to make a completely new color!

1 Fill two glasses with water. Place an empty glass between them.

2 Put five drops of yellow food coloring into the glass on the left and five drops of blue food coloring into the glass on the right.

10

3 Roll up two sheets of paper towels. Take one of the rolled-up paper towels and place one end in the glass of yellow water. Put the other end into the empty glass.

4 Take the other paper towel and place one end in the glass of blue water and the other end in the empty glass.

5 Watch the glasses closely.

▶ **What do you think might happen in the middle glass?**

Write your predictions in your notebook.

In your notebook, record what happened.

▶ **What did you see in the middle glass?**

▶ **Do you predictions match what happened?**

▶ **What happens if you mix blue and yellow paints together?**

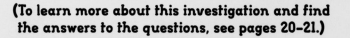

(To learn more about this investigation and find the answers to the questions, see pages 20–21.)

What makes up different colors?

Paint colors can be made by mixing different colors together. The same is true for markers. While some markers contain **ink** that's just one color, other marker colors are created by mixing two or more ink colors. We can't see the different colors just by looking at the marker. You can separate the different colored inks in markers, though, by doing this next experiment. Let's investigate!

You will need:

- Scissors
- A paper towel
- A baking pan
- Different colored markers
- Tape
- A pitcher of water
- A notebook and pencil

 Cut a paper towel into a strip that is six inches (15 cm) wide and the length of a baking pan.

six inches (15 cm)

2 About half an inch (1 cm) from the edge of the paper, gently press different-colored markers onto the paper towel to make large dots of color.

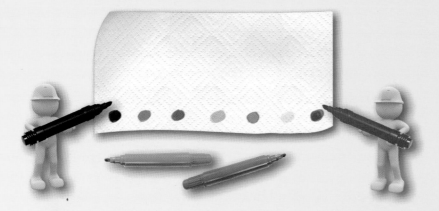

3 Tape the paper towel into the baking pan, with the dots at the bottom. The edge of the paper towel should be about half an inch (1 cm) from the bottom of the pan.

tape

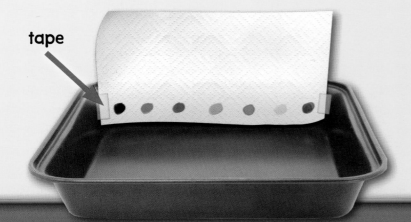

4 Slowly pour water into the pan. The water should be high enough to just touch the edge of the paper towel.

5 Soon, the paper towel will start to soak up the water.

Carefully watch the dots and record everything you observe.

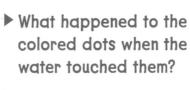

▶ What happened to the colored dots when the water touched them?

▶ What colors did you see spreading from each dot?

▶ Does every marker color contain different colors?

(To learn more about this investigation and find the answers to the questions, see pages 20–21.)

How can we make colors lighter or darker?

Find some objects that are green. What do you notice about the color green? Like many colors, it's not just one color. There are many different **shades** of green. For example, there is dark green and pale green. Let's investigate how colors can be different shades.

You will need:

- Green leaves
- Liquid paint, including green, white, and black
- A notebook and pencil
- A teaspoon and a white dish (for mixing paint)

1 In a garden or park, collect leaves that are many different shades of green.

Look for green leaves that have fallen to the ground. If you want to remove a leaf from a plant, ask a grown-up for help.

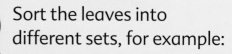

2 Sort the leaves into different sets, for example:

- dark green
- pale green
- bright green

Compare the colors of your leaves to some green paint.

▶ Are the shades of the leaves a darker green or lighter green than your paint?

▶ Can you describe the shades of green using other colors? For example, is a leaf a yellowish green or a brownish green?

yellowish green

brownish green

Choose one of the leaves and try to match its color using paint.

To make a paint color lighter, mix in some white paint.

To make a color darker, mix in black.

▶ To match the color of your leaf, do you think you will need to add white or black paint to the green paint? What about other colors?

Write your predictions in your notebook.

Mix your paints using a teaspoon and a white dish.

Remember, if your color doesn't match the leaf, you can always start again with some fresh green paint.

▶ What colors did you add to the green paint?

▶ Do your predictions match what happened?

▶ Did you make the same shade of green as the leaf or did you make a completely new shade of green?

(To learn more about this investigation and find the answers to the questions, see pages 20–21.)

15

How can we invent new colors?

You've tried mixing paints to create a shade of green. Now use your imagination to **invent** a new paint color! The new color can be made using any combination of paints. As you're making your color, be sure to keep a careful record of every step. Then you can write a **recipe** for your new color that another person can follow. Let's get started!

You will need:

- A notebook and pencil
- A teaspoon
- Liquid paints
- A white dish
- An eyedropper

 Begin by thinking about colors.

▶ What's your favorite color?

▶ Would you like your new color to be a shade of your favorite color?

▶ Will your new color be light or dark?

Write your ideas in your notebook.

2 Put a teaspoon of paint in a white dish.

Remember to record each step in your notebook.

3 Now add other colors to your mixture using the teaspoon. Be sure to clean the teaspoon before using it again.

To add small amounts of paint, use an eyedropper.

Write down which colors you use and the exact amounts.

4 After you've made your new color, name it. If the color reminds you of something, include it in the color's name. For example:

• chocolate pudding brown
• stormy sky blue
• tomato ketchup red

Carefully write out the recipe for mixing your new paint color.

Now follow your recipe and make your color again.

▶ Does the color look exactly the same?

▶ If not, what do you think you did differently?

(To learn more about this investigation and find the answers to the questions, see pages 20–21.)

17

How do animals use color to stay safe?

The color of some animals' fur or skin helps them match their surroundings. This is called **camouflage**. For many animals, it's important to blend into their **habitat** in order to stay safe from **predators**. Sometimes, an animal's camouflage is not very colorful. Other animals, however, have very colorful camouflage that can even be more than one color. Let's investigate how camouflage works.

You will need:

- A sheet of white paper
- Scissors
- Crayons, colored pencils, or markers
- Clear tape
- A notebook and pencil

a chameleon

a moth

1 You are going to use camouflage to hide a circle of paper in your room.

Begin by finding a colorful object or section of a wall.

This is where you will hide your circle.

2 Cut a circle of white paper that is about two inches (5 cm) across.

Color the circle using crayons, colored pencils, or markers so that it matches the colors of the object or hiding place.

3 Tape the circle to the object or hiding place. Now ask a friend to be a predator.

Your friend must stand in the center of the room and try to spot the circle.

▶ Did your friend find it easy or difficult to find the circle? Why?

Once your friend has found the hiding place, try again with a different hiding place and circle.

Try to make a circle that has such good camouflage your friend can't find it.

Write down your observations in your notebook.

(To learn more about this investigation and find the answers to the questions, see pages 20–21.)

Discovery Time

It's fun to investigate the world using science! Now let's check out all the amazing things we discovered about color.

Pages 6-7

What makes a rainbow?

The water in the glass caused the light to bend and split into different colors—just like raindrops bend and split sunlight.

The different colors of light formed a rainbow on the paper.

Pages 8-9

Can different colors make things warmer?

The water in the glass wrapped in black paper is hotter than the water in the glass wrapped in white paper. That's because the black paper absorbed more heat than the white paper.

When sunlight hit the white paper, it was reflected, or bounced away.

Dark colors absorb heat and light colors reflect heat.

To stay cooler on a hot day, wear a white or light-colored T-shirt that will not absorb heat.

Pages 10-11

How can we make new colors?

The paper towels soaked up the water, which then moved up the towels and collected in the middle cup.

The water in the middle cup turned green because it was a mixture of blue and yellow water.

When blue and yellow paints are mixed together, they make green.

What makes up different colors?

When the water touches the colored dots, the ink spreads out through the paper.

As the ink spreads, it separates into the different colored inks that are used to make the marker colors.

Some colors, however, are made from just one color.

Pages 12-13

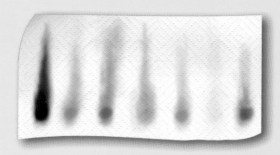

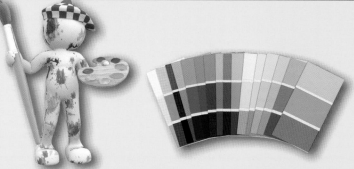

How can we make colors lighter or darker?

The shade of a paint color can be made lighter by adding white paint.

Adding black paint makes the color darker.

It's possible to make thousands of different shades of a paint color by adding white, black, and other colors.

Pages 14-15

How can we invent new colors?

Did you have fun inventing a new paint color?

You can make the same color again and again using your recipe. Your recipe is a record of what you did.

Keeping records is an important part of being a scientist.

Scientists record all the things they do and observe during an experiment so another scientist can do the same experiment in the future.

Pages 16-17

How do animals use color to stay safe?

Camouflage helps protect animals by allowing them to blend into their habitat. Camouflage also helps some predators to sneak up on their prey. For example, a polar bear's fur is white like the snow where it lives. The bear's camouflage helps it blend into its snowy surroundings as it hunts for seals.

Pages 18-19

Colors in Your World

Now that you've made discoveries about color, look out for different colors in your world. Be a scientist and inventor with your paints!

1. On a sunny day, spray water from a hose into the air where there is sunlight.

▶ **What can you see in the drops of water?**

2. In countries where it's hot, such as Greece, people paint their houses white.

▶ **Why do you think they do this?**

3. Next time you are painting, try mixing new colors.

▶ **What color do you get if you mix red and blue paint?**

4. During the summer, sit in a grassy area and keep watch for grasshoppers.

▶ **Why do you think grasshoppers are green?**

5. Colors can come in many different shades.

▶ **How many objects can you find in your home that are different shades of red?**

Answers: 1. The water from the hose acts like raindrops. It bends the sunlight and splits the colors of the rainbow. 2. Just like a white T-shirt, a white house will reflect sunlight. In hot countries, painting a house white helps to keep it cool inside. 3. If you mix red and blue paint, you get purple. 4. Many types of grasshoppers are green. Their green color is camouflage that makes it hard for predators, such as birds, to see them on green plants. 5. In your home, you might find apples, tomatoes, peppers, clothes, and toys.

Science Words

absorb (ab-ZORB) to soak up something

camouflage (KAM-uh-flahzh) colors and markings on an animal's body that help it blend in with its surroundings

habitat (HAB-uh-tat) a place in nature where a plant or animal normally lives

ink (INGK) a coloring used in markers, pens, and printers

invent (in-VENT) to make something or think of an idea

predators (PRED-uh-turz) animals that hunt and eat other animals

predictions (pri-DIK-shuhns) guesses that something will happen in a certain way; they are often based on facts a person knows or something a person has observed

rainbow (RAYN-*boh*) a curved, colorful shape in the sky formed when sunlight is bent by raindrops

recipe (RESS-i-pee) a set of step-by-step instructions for making something

shades (SHAYDZ) different versions of colors that may be dark or light

temperature (TEMP-pur-uh-chur) a measurement of how hot or cold something is

thermometer (thur-MOM-uh-tur) an instrument used to measure temperature

Index

camouflage 18–19, 21, 22

heat 8–9, 20, 22

inks 12–13, 21

leaves 14–15

light 5, 6–7, 20, 22

paint 10–11, 14–15, 16–17, 20–21, 22

rainbows 5, 6–7, 20, 22

shades 14–15, 21, 22

sunlight 5, 6, 8–9, 20, 22

Read More

Lawrence, Ellen. *A Chameleon's Life (Animal Diaries: Life Cycles).* New York: Bearport (2013).

René, Ellen. *Investigating Why Leaves Change Their Color (Science Detectives).* New York: Rosen (2009).

Shields, Amy. *Little Kids First Big Book of Why.* Washington, DC: National Geographic (2011).

Learn More Online

To learn more about color, visit
www.bearportpublishing.com/FundamentalExperiments

About the Author

Ellen Lawrence lives in the United Kingdom. Her favorite books to write are those about nature and animals. In fact, the first book Ellen bought for herself, when she was six years old, was the story of a gorilla named Patty Cake that was born in New York's Central Park Zoo.